THE QUESTION IS

"WOULD IT MAKE A DIFFERENCE IF THEY WERE HUMAN?"

essential reading
for every literate individual in the world

CAROL ELIZABETH MOSCA

ISBN 978-1-484-15888-3

This book is dedicated to
all sentient nonhuman beings
who are legally regarded as property,
and
all African Americans
who were legally regarded as property.

Contents

Contents

continued

Forward

"Never doubt that a small group of thoughtfully committed
citizens can change the world;
indeed, it's the only thing that ever has."
Margaret Mead, American cultural anthropologist,
1901-1978

Since the beginning of time, individuals have left profound effects on future ages by overcoming criticism, persecution and accusations of heresy in order to change traditions, thoughts and ideas of cultures throughout the world which include the following landmark accomplishments.

Aristole's (384-322 BC) ancient physics and Aristarchus of Samos's (work circa 275 BC) heliocentric hypothesis of the earth revolving around the sun which confounded tradition eventually served as the basis for the work of Nicolaus Copernicus (1473-1543) and Galileo Galilei (1564-1642) during the seventeenth century Scientific Revolution which shifted the world view that an infinite, orderly cosmos appealing to human reason and empirical evidence replaced the medieval vision of a closed universe centered on a stationary earth permeating with Christian purpose.(1)(2)

Alexandrians in Greece dissected human cadavers despite their religious belief that prohibited mutilation of dead bodies which led to physician Herophilus of Chalcedon's (circa 320-250 BC) discovery that the brain is the center of the nervous system which served as a key to advancement in medicine.(3)

Jesus of Nazareth introduced Christianity to Palestine which eventually and unexpectedly replaced paganism as the official religion of the Roman Empire.(4)

In 1429, Joan of Arc (died 1431) assisted the King of France in driving out the English. Although she was condemned and burned as a heretic by the English in 1431, Pope Calixtus III reversed the condemnation in 1456, and in 1920, she was canonized as the patron Saint of France.(5)

In 1859 and 1871 respectively, Charles Darwin (1809-1882) published *On the Origin of the Species by Means or Natural Selection* and *Descent of Man* in which he recognized that human beings were members of the animal kingdom like other species which appeared to undermine orthodox religious certainties by illustrating their incompatibility with scientific discoveries.(6)

In 1861, the institution of human slavery in America was abolished.

In 1920, the Nineteenth Constitutional Amendment for women's suffrage in America was ratified.

Introduction

In its most simplistic form, this e-book represents a survey of the reasons notable academicians advise human beings to exercise Wisdom and Compassion by practicing the following acts:

‡ Avoid skin, flesh, milk and eggs derived from sentient nonhuman beings.

‡ Purchase faux fur, wool, leather, feathers, and other synthetic materials.

‡ Boycott *anything and everything* that is tested on sentient nonhuman beings.

‡ Boycott events in which sentient nonhuman beings serve as subjects of entertainment.

If you don't do it for the animals, do it for your health;
If you don't do it for your health, do it for the environment;
If you don't do it for the environment, do it for the global poor.

This survey/book represents "A Voice for the Voiceless" and an appeal to common sense. It was re-searched and written out of Love, compassion and heartfelt concern for *all* living, breathing, sentient nonhuman beings and *not* for the intent or residual purpose/design to offend human beings. The target audience is the common masses, individuals of diverse backgrounds and cultures. Accordingly, it should be read with an open mind in order to understand the *logic of the argument* as well as an open heart and intellect to comprehend the critical issues regarding the billions of innocent, sacred, precious lives at stake every year.

This book concerns ethics, morality and compassion regarding nonhuman civil rights. Although nonhuman beings *arguably may not* possess the cognitive abilities to reason as do human beings, they do possess sentience (the capability of feeling; consciousness) which qualifies nonhuman beings to represent members of the moral community. Nonhuman beings are entitled to The Right not to be regarded as property. They deserve equal consideration to human beings because they possess sentience; they have a morally significant interest in continuing their lives without suffering as do *human* beings. They should not be regarded as property which extends to the subsidiary right of not being exploited by human beings.

Sentience is the exclusive, necessary and sufficient condition for the possession of rights to life, liberty and freedom not to be used as commodities or resources of other sentient beings. Since animal welfare laws have tragically failed to adequately protect the interests and lives of sentient nonhuman beings, the only feasible solution remains Veganism, the *abolition of the use of all products derived from sentient nonhuman beings*, the moral baseline of Animal Rights.

In the aftermath of the tragedy of 911, American citizens sacrificed freedom for security. During the last decade in the United States, the socio-economic, political climate has inherited socialistic characteristics that remain quite distinguishable from the original understanding and meaning of the political philosophy of the Framers. The combination of the two aforementioned events has served as the impetus of a myriad of controversial legislation and highlighted the poignant legal arena of the protection of Civil Rights and Liberties. This intriguing area of law addresses unchartered territory with each progressive wave of ideas and issues that change traditions and result in landmark legal decisions. Of all the issues that arguably have the potential to relate to Civil Rights and Liberties, the most advanced is that of Animal Rights, ie, the concept of personhood (that animals should not be regarded as property) and legal rights regarding animals.

With respect to legislation, the fact of the matter is that morality has always been legislated. (Laws against hate speech, drug use, slavery, rape, incest, pedophilia, murder and prostitution have been successfully passed throughout the decades.) As the animal liberation movement progresses, world renowned academicians advocate for Animal Rights. "Speciesism," ie, discrimination based on species, or some construction thereof, awaits legislative success because nonhuman animals, like all sentient beings, deserve the rights to life, liberty and freedom not to be used as commodities or resources of human beings.

The application of Civil Rights and Liberties to Animal Law has already made its debut in federal court. On February 8, 2012, the United States District Court, Southern District of California, decided *TILIKUM, Katina, Corky, Kasatka, and Ulises, five orcas, by their Next Friends, PEOPLE FOR THE ETHICAL TREATMENT OF*

ANIMALS, INC., Richard "Ric" O'Barry, Ingrid N. Visser, Ph.D., Howard Garrrett, Samantha Berg, and Carol Ray v. SEA WORLD PARKS & ENTERTAINMENT, INC. and Sea World, LLC, Case No. 3:11-CV-02476-JM-WMC, an action based on the Thirteenth Amendment of the Constitution which prohibits slavery and involuntary servitude. Although the Court dismissed the case for lack of subject matter jurisdiction, the action remains an impermeable representation of real life ideas and controversies in today's world.

Amazingly, moral issues regarding sentient nonhuman beings and their rights originated in ancient times. The most extensive and stately ancient account was that of the Neoplatonist philosopher Porphyry (circa 3rd-4th century AD) in his influential treatise *On Abstinence from Animal Food*.(7) The first "modern" discussion is *Historical and Critical Dictionary* (originally published in 1697) authored by French philosopher Pierre Bayle. Bayle's enlightening work cites ancient, medieval and modern authors "who discuss whether animals have souls, whether they deserve some form of moral consideration, and whether animals reason."(8)

The aforementioned epoch-making moral and ethical issue of the status of sentient nonhuman beings in society continued with the writings of Jeremy Bentham (1748-1832) and his notable quotation, "[T]he question is not, 'Can they *reason?*' nor 'Can they *talk?*' but, 'Can they *suffer?*'" Although Dr. Jane Goodall, United Nations Messenger of Peace, Founder of the Jane Goodall Institute and author of *The Chimpanzees of Gombe* published by Harvard University Press (among other enlightening works) began a trailblazing, field study of the behavior of chimpanzees in Tanzania, Africa in 1960, the animal rights movement did not gain momentum until Peter Singer, Ira W. DeCamp Professor of Bioethics at Princeton University's Center for Human Values, published an evolutionary work entitled *Animal Liberation* (9) in 1975.

Today, the emerging field of "Animal Law" represents one of the newest and most progressive legal arenas, but, as the pioneer of the Animal Rights position, Gary L. Francione, Distinguished Professor of Law and Nicholas deB. Katzenback Scholar of Law and Philosophy (10) keenly recognizes, the study and practice of Animal Law has unfortunately denigrated to a subsidiary of Property

Law with specialization in custody of animals during marriage dissolution and related matters. In stark contrast, the intrinsic issue of Animal Law remains the *moral consideration* of sentient nonhuman beings in society today, the identical point Bayle raised more than 300 years ago and ancient philosophers implied over 2,000 years ago.

This survey/book does not represent an outstanding literary or artistic work in the most remote sense. Rather, it serves as a compilation of ideas, research and personal accounts of the leading academicians and praiseworthy advocates of the animal liberation movement. It is a fervent call for *understanding*.

Accordingly, it is the author's hope that every literate individual in the world will *understand* the urgent need for animal rights, feel compelled to learn more about the significance and ramifications of this issue by reading the books listed in the bibliography herein (or learning about the topics in school), and develop a passionate desire to act as the time is ripe for *serious action*.

"Only if we understand can we care.

Only if we care will we help.

Only if we help shall they be saved."

Jane Goodall

1 / Animals Rights verses Animal Welfare

Generally speaking, in the most simplistic form, there exist two ideologies within the animal liberation movement—Animal Rights which focuses on the *use* of animals and Animal Welfare which concerns *treatment* of animals. The purpose of this "survey" book is to advocate the Animal Rights position in a fundamental manner to appeal to a diversified audience because, as an advanced society, we remain seriously delinquent in taking action to effectively end abuse, neglect, torture and cruelty of sentient nonhuman beings.

The pioneer of the Animal Rights position is Gary L. Francione, Distinguished Professor of Law and Nicholas deB. Katzenback Scholar of Law and Philosophy. In 1985, Professor Francione ingeniously advocated his Abolitionist Theory of Animal Rights exclusively based on sentience

1

(the capability of feeling; consciousness) and began teaching Animal Rights Theory as part of his course in Jurisprudence at University of Pennsylvania Law School, representing the first Animal Law Professor in the United States. From 1990-2000, Professor Francione and colleague, Anna Charlton, operated the nation's first Animal Rights Law Clinic at Rutgers University School of Law.

Professor Francione's Abolitionist Theory of Animal Rights, The Right not to be regarded as property, qualifies nonhuman beings to represent members of the moral community. They deserve equal consideration because they possess sentience (which includes self awareness); they have a morally significant interest in continuing their lives without suffering as do *human* beings.

Veganism, the *abolition of the use of all products derived from sentient nonhuman beings*, is the moral baseline of Animal Rights. See Professor Francione's website www.AbolitionistApproach.com.

In contrast, Animal Welfare regulates the treatment of sentient nonhuman beings to make exploitation more "humane." One of its greatest accomplishments remains the perpetuation of enormous distress, pain and suffering of sentient nonhuman beings by protecting economic and legal interests of the exploiters.

The Animal Welfare Act (AWA) as Amended (7 USC, 2131-2159) "requires that *minimum* standards of care and treatment are provided for certain animals bred for commercial sale, used in research, transported commercially or exhibited in public." Accordingly, AWA serves as detrimental guidelines to the well being of sentient nonhuman animals.

Specifically, AWA does not protect sentient nonhuman beings during experiments regardless of how painful or unnecessary the experiments are. No regulations exist to govern the conduct of experiments or the level of torture that sentient nonhuman beings are forced to endure, and AWA does not include rats and mice who represent the largest lot of victims in this arena. In addition, AWA gives sentient nonhuman beings *minimum* protection for handling, care, housing, treatment, ventilation, lighting, shelter, veterinary care and separation by species. An example of "*minimum* standard" means that the sizes of the sentient nonhuman animals' cages need to provide them only the ability to turn around. In general, "*minimum* standards" are based on the discretion of USDA inspectors. Shockingly, AWA permits cruel, horrific abuse and neglect of institutionalized sentient nonhuman beings—acts that warrant criminal charges when performed by private citizens and that would likely be regarded as torture if they were committed against human beings.

Enforcement of AWA has been deficient and difficult at best. Constant problems of reporting violations and imposing fines for violations have been documented over the last several decades. Although the Humane Society of the United States has made progress with respect to the United States Department of Agriculture (USDA) resuming the posting of electronic Freedom of Information Act (E-FOIA) summaries of inspection reports on their website in keeping with translucency in government, the magnitude of the dismal failure of AWA is evidenced by the lack of disclosure of the number of sentient nonhuman beings housed at particular facilities, inspection policies that allow licensees to operate indefinitely with documented violations of AWA regulations and standards, and in the rare instances in which USDA authorities prosecute AWA violators, judges routinely impose fines and/or penalties at fractions of the level authorized by statutes.

Most unconscionably and significantly, AWA represents a dispiriting failure in that its greatest accomplishments thus far represent protraction of federal programs that waste tax dollars, *and* perpetuation of enormous distress, pain and suffering of sentient nonhuman beings by protecting the exploiters' economic and legal interests.

2 / A Case for Animal Rights

♥ Sentience

Sentience is the capability of feeling. Sentience represents the exclusive requirement for consciousness. All animals, both human and nonhuman, possess sentience because all animals have the ability to experience feelings of joy, happiness, pain, sadness, depression and loneliness. Nonhuman beings, like human beings, have the right not to be regarded as property and to represent members of the moral community based on sentience alone.

Jeremy Bentham (1748-1832) recognized that nonhuman beings possess sentience and famously stated, "[T]he question is not, 'Can they *reason?*' nor 'Can they *talk?*' but, 'Can they *suffer?*'"

In *The Descent of Man*, Charles Darwin states,

I fully subscribe to the judgment of those writers who maintain that of all the differences between man and the lower animals, the moral sense or conscience is by far the most important.(11)

Darwin argues that nonhuman animals have emotions such as love and sympathy, both for their kin and their larger social group. They have social instincts, enjoy companions, are sympathetic with the plight of those to whom they are close, help their fellows, knowingly risk their lives, grieve in the loss of life, and are gratified by others' approval of their behavior.(12)

Most notably, three world renowned academicians support the aforementioned perceptions of sentience, ie, conscience, with respect to nonhuman beings.

In 1960, Jane Goodall, United Nations Messenger of Peace, Founder of the Jane Goodall Institute and author of *The Chimpanzees of Gombe* published by Harvard University Press (among other enlightening works), began her groundbreaking, field study of the behavior of chimpanzees in Tanzania, Africa (which started with a valuable contribution to science, ie, recorded, personal observations of chimpanzees using tools). In *Through a Window, My Thirty Years with the Chimpanzees of Gombe*, Jane Goodall prolifically stated, "When I began my observations in 1960, it was still commonly believed that there was a difference of kind, not just degree, separating humans and the rest of the animal kingdom, that there was a sharp line between us and them. Chimpanzees were used in medical research...because (it was asserted) they, unlike us, did not have personalities...or emotions."(13)

In 1975, Peter Singer, Ira W. DeCamp Professor of Bioethics at Princeton University's Center for Human Values, advocated respect for the well being and lives of nonhuman animals because nonhuman beings possess sentience. Professor Singer brilliantly and logically proved that nonhuman beings possess sentience in his infamous work entitled *Animal Liberation*. Since 1975, Professor Singer published several editions of his enlightening book including the most recent updated version, *Animal Liberation, The Definitive Classic of the Animal Movement*. [This work provides a comprehensive history of unconscionable exploitation of sentient nonhuman beings beginning with research and experimentation by the United States Department of Defense, universities (dating as far back as 1933) and corporations to present day factory farming and the entertainment industry.]

In *Animal Liberation*, Professor Singer explains that if a living being suffers, there can be no moral justification for refusing to take that suffering into consideration. All animals feel pain. "The behavioral signs include writhing, facial contortions, moaning, yelping or other forms of calling, attempts to avoid the source of pain, appearance of fear and terror at the prospect of its repetition, screaming, crying, trying to physically escape."(14) There is no good reason to deny that animals feel pain. Since nonhuman beings generally possess keener, more acute senses than human beings, they may feel *more* than human beings. There exists no moral justification for regarding the pain (or pleasure) that nonhuman beings feel as less important than the same amount of pain felt by human beings.(15)

Professor Singer expounds that if sentient human beings feel pain, then sentient nonhuman beings do also because both species possess nervous systems. Both sentient human and sentient nonhuman beings have "nervous systems which provide physiological signs of pain: an initial rise in blood pressure, dilated pupils, perspiration and increased pulse rate, and if the stimulus continues, a fall in blood pressure."(16) Professor Singer notes that, as Jane Goodall pointed out in her study of chimpanzees, *In the Shadow of Man*, "when it comes to expression of feelings and emotions, language is less important than nonlinguistic modes of communication such as cheering, a pat on the back, an exuberant embrace, a clasp of hands, etc. The basic signals we use to convey pain, fear, anger, love, joy, surprise, sexual arousal and many other emotional states are not specific to our own species."(17)

The most profound theses exist in the brilliant works of Professor Gary L. Francione.

> Sentience is 'the necessary and sufficient condition for the possession of rights. Specifically, [Professor Francione] argues that all sentient beings, those capable of experiencing pleasure and pain, have a fundamental interest in avoiding suffering and continuing to exist.'(18)

> [A]ny being that is sentient necessarily has an interest in life because sentience is a means to the end of continued existence....[T]his being also has a right to life and the avoidance of suffering that is equal in principle to the right to life enjoyed

10

by any other sentient being....If a being has a right to life, then that being also has a right not to be property. This right is basic in the sense that it gives rise to important subsidiary rights, such as the right not to be killed for food, experimented upon, or used for entertainment....[T]hese rights are shared equally by human and nonhuman animals; they have a categorical force that forbids us to subordinate the interests and fortunes of animals to those of humans.(19)

♥ Animal Welfare laws have Failed to Significantly Protect Sentient Nonhuman Beings

The animal protection organization, People for the Ethical Treatment of Animals (PETA), has contributed to the animal liberation movement, most notably, by conducting undercover investigations of unconscionable acts of inhumane, cruel, torturous treatment of *unanesthetized* sentient nonhuman beings in the factory farming industries of food, clothing and other consumer products such as furniture, carpeting, et al., research and experimentation fields as well as the entertainment arena, and uploading the horrific results on its world renowned website, www.peta.org. See also Mercy for Animals' website www.chooseveg.com, accounts of undercover investigations in Kathy Freston's *Veganist, Lose Weight, Get Healthy, Change the World*(20), and graphic detail in Peter Singer's *Animal Liberation* and Tom L. Beauchamp, et al.'s *The Human Use of Animals, Case Studies in Ethical Choice.*

Tragically for the innocent sentient nonhuman victims, PETA's dedication and due diligence has, to date,

12

merely accomplished making exploitation more "humane" through subtle and insignificant revisions of the Animal Welfare Act, other animal welfare laws and industry standards.

Professor Francione correctly exhorts,

[T]he property status of animals means that the level of protection provided by these laws and standards generally does not go beyond what is necessary to exploit the animals efficiently. We generally protect animal interests only to the extent we derive an economic benefit from doing so.(21)

Although the animal welfare paradigm has prevailed for some two hundred years, we are using more animals than ever before in human history and we still 'torment' them.(22)

[W]elfarist regulation does not significantly protect nonhumans in the short term, does not lead to abolition in the long term, and only facilitates social comfort with and acceptance of animal use.(23)

An act, 'which inflicts pain, even the great pain of mutilation, and which is cruel in the ordinary sense of the word' is not prohibited

13

'[w]henever the purpose of which the act is done is to make the animal more serviceable for the use of man.' For example, courts have held consistently that animals used for food may be mutilated in ways that unquestionably cause severe pain and suffering and that would normally be regarded as cruel or even as torture. These practices are permitted, however, because animal agriculture is an accepted institutionalized animal use, and those in the meat industry regard the practices as normal and necessary to facilitate that use. Courts often presume that animal owners will act in their best economic interests and will not intentionally inflict more suffering than is necessary on an animal because to do so would diminish the monetary value of the animal. For example, in *Callaghan v. Society for the Prevention of Cruelty to Animals,* the court held that the painful act of dehorning cattle did not constitute unnecessary abuse because farmers would not perform this procedure if it were not necessary. The self-interest of the farmer would prevent the infliction of 'useless pain or torture,' which 'would necessarily reduce the condition of the animal; and unless they very soon recovered, the farmer would lose in the sale.'(24)

[Likewise], [s]lave welfare laws failed for precisely the same reason that animal welfare laws fail to establish any meaningful limit on our use of animal property. The owner's property interest in the slave always trumped any interest of the slave who was ostensibly protected under the law. The interests of slaves were observed only when it provided economic benefit for the owners or served their whim.(25)

Because animals are property, we consider as 'humane' treatment that we would regard as torture if it were inflicted on humans....For example, the federal Humane Slaughter Act, which supposedly requires the 'humane' slaughter of nonhumans for food purposes, prohibits suffering only to the extent that it ensures worker safety, reduces carcass damage, and provides other economic benefits for humans. It would, however, be an absurd use of the word to characterize any slaughterhouse as humane.'(26)

Battery hens that supply some of the the major fast-food chains may now live in an area equivalent to a square of approximately 8.5 inches rather than the average industry standard—a square of approximately 7.8 inches—but it would be nonsense to claim that the existence of a battery hen in the larger cage is anything but miserable. Indeed, 'cage free' hens are often packed together so tightly in sheds that they are crushed and have very limited movement.(27)

Accordingly, the three most important considerations of institutionalized use of sentient nonhuman beings remain speedy production, worker safety and profit.

♥ Ethics, Morality and Compassion

"If we eat the flesh of living creatures,
we are destroying the seeds of compassion."
From the Surangama Sutra

[T]he principle problem is not *how* we use animals but *that* we use animals for human purposes at all. We have no moral justification for using nonhumans, however 'humanely' we treat them. To the extent that we do use animals, it is, of course, always better to cause less pain than more pain. It is better that a rapist not torture the victim in addition to committing the rape. But just as it is not morally acceptable to commit rape even if you do not torture the victim, it is not morally acceptable to use nonhumans as human resources despite how we treat them.(28)

It would, however, be morally repugnant to maintain that we can be 'conscientious rapists' by ensuring that we not beat rape victims. Similarly, it is disturbing that animal advocates are promoting the notion that we can be morally 'conscientious omnivores' if we eat the supposedly 'humanely' produced products.(29)

17

[I]f our use of animals is not morally justifiable, promoting more 'humane' exploitation as a means to the end of abolition is unacceptable as a matter of moral theory. For example, if we believe that any form of pedophilia is morally wrong, we cannot, consistent with that position, campaign for 'humane' pedophilia. In the struggle against human slavery in the United States, many of those who favored abolition refused to campaign for the reform of slavery because they considered reform as inconsistent with the basic moral principle that slavery was an inherently unjust institution. Similarly, the promotion of a more 'humane' animal use is inconsistent with the idea that we do not have a moral right to exploit animals in the first place.(30)

"A good deed done to an animal is as meritorious

as a good deed done to a human being,

while an act of cruelty to an animal is as bad

as an act of cruelty to a human being."

Mohammed, 570-632

18

Food

"I have from an early age abjured the use of meat.
And the time will come when men such as I
will look upon the murder of animals
the way we now look upon the murder of men."
Leonardo Da Vinci, 1452-1519

[W]e kill billions of animals every year for food. It is certainly not necessary for us to eat animal flesh, dairy, eggs, or other animal products; indeed, the evidence is mounting that animal foods are detrimental to human health. Moreover, animal agriculture is an ecological disaster. The only justification that we have for using animals in this way is that we are accustomed to and enjoy the taste of meat and animal products. The welfare position does not challenge our use of animals for food and says only that we should not inflict more suffering than is necessary when we use animals for this unnecessary purpose. But what does 'necessary' mean in this context, given that *no* suffering is necessary because we have no need to eat meat or animal products?(31)

[E]ven the most 'humane' nations treat animals who are used for food in ways that

19

would be considered torture if humans were so treated.(32)

"If slaughterhouses had glass walls,

everyone would be vegetarian.

We feel better about ourselves and better about the

animals knowing we're not contributing to their pain."

Sir Paul and Linda McCartney

Of all the animals commonly eaten in the Western world, the pig is without doubt the most intelligent. The natural intelligence of a pig is comparable and perhaps even superior to that of a dog; it is possible to rear pigs as companions to human beings and train them to respond to simple commands much as a dog would.(33)

[Despite the intelligence and social ability of pigs], [b]acon, pork chops, ham, sausage, hot dogs, bratwurst, tenderloin, ribs, pork roast, pulled-pork sandwiches, and pepperoni pizza...Pigs are the largest single source of meat for human beings, accounting for almost 40% of meat consumption worldwide by weight. Each year in the United States, over 100 million pigs are slaughtered, for total cash receipts in excess of $10 billion.(34)

Most consumers of pig meat have no contact with the animals they eat and little if any knowledge of the conditions under which the animals are raised and slaughtered....The Humane Farming Association (HFA) has obtained video footage of pigs being boiled alive, beaten, and killed without being stunned or otherwise rendered insensitive to pain.(35)

Joe Suing, former manager of HKY, a large hog farm located in Wausa, Nebraska invited representatives from HFA to visit the farm before he quit in 2004 after several unsuccessful attempts to compel the farm to meet legal standards.

According to HFA chief investigator Gail Eisnitz, 'On its face, this evidence documents a pervasive pattern of unconscionable abuse affecting thousands of animals. In addition, to unspeakable cruelty, there exists a serious threat to public health because pigs from this filthy, disease-ridden operation are being sold to one of the largest suppliers of pork in the country.'(36)

"Since visiting the abbatoirs [slaughterhouses] of South France, I have stopped eating meat."
Vincent Van Gogh, 1853-1890

In September 2004, Josh Balk worked undercover at a chicken factory on behalf of the organization Compassion over Killing.

> While I had seen plenty of animal slaughter footage, I had never experienced how truly horrific and heartbreaking the process was until I witnessed firsthand as an employee at this plant.
> Speed was the most important objective, since our workday ended once a quota was achieved.
> Many of the chickens responded with screams and violent physical reactions from the moment the workers grabbed them.
> While working there I tried to hang the birds as gently as possible, which made me slower than my co-workers.
> Even if every worker handled the animals with the utmost care—which would be impossible, because of the speed of the kill lines—the birds would still suffer dramatically because of the unnaturally rapid growth that increases the chance of skeletal and muscular problems; the transport from the factory farms to the slaughterhouse where they're packed into small cages; the dumping of them on a conveyor belt from their transport trucks; the shackling of their legs into metal restraints; the slicing of their necks while they're fully conscious; and the

drowning in scalding tanks for those birds who don't have their throats cut.

It's shameful that while we take so much from these animals, we can't even afford them a less-cruel death. Chickens have the same spark of life as our pets at home. They have the same desire to avoid suffering and follow their nature. Yet, we treat chickens so cruelly that similar abuses inflicted upon dogs or cats would warrant criminal charges.(37)

In January and February 2008, Nathan Runkle from the nonprofit Mercy for Animals worked undercover at one of California's largest egg farms. He shared this observation among graphic detail of horrific mistreatment of hens.

The workers were supposed to kill the hens by breaking their necks, in either of two methods. The more common method was pulling the hens' necks until the vertebrae separated. A worker demonstrated the technique by pulling a hen's head while he held her body under one armpit. She flapped her wings and kicked her legs frantically.

[H]e would leave them on the floor, unable to move, to be collected later. I found some inside the trash cans used to collect dead chickens—live, breathing birds buried underneath the dead.

Bird injuries and neglect were common at the farm. I remember coming across one bird that had a wound I can only describe as a crater in her side...missing most of her feathers on her exposed right side. She didn't move as I lifted her...examining a wound about three inches across her torso. It was sunken in at the center and built up around the edges, openly bleeding in several areas. I set her on the floor, where she lay without opening her eyes or lifting her head....She counted as nothing now...I wondered how long she had endured her current state, and how much pain it took to keep her from opening her eyes and calling out. I imagined she was dehydrated and starving from being unable to stand and get food or water, but figured that was a minor discomfort compared to the pain of an infected, open wound that crippled her. I wanted to help her; I wanted to take her from the farm and try to have her healed. That would not be possible, I knew.(38)

In December 2008, Runkle was hired as a maintenance worker on a large dairy farm. He shared this story among massive abuses he witnessed during his six week tenure.

24

Number 70426, a four-year-old Holstein cow, has just begun to give birth. A worker arrives carrying an archaic-looking metal device that he clamps between the mother cow's nostrils, tethering her in place. He then walks behind her and wraps a steel chain around the emerging forelegs of the birthing calf, putting all of his weight into yanking it out.

The calf falls to the ground with a thud and lies startled on the barren concrete floor....Once the worker releases 70426, she makes a beeline directly to her newborn calf, contentedly comforting her with gentle licks. This heartwarming scene is interrupted after only mere minutes, when the worker returns, abruptly grabs the calf and begins to drag her away by one hind leg.

Number 70426 runs behind her calf as they each bellow in distress. When the calf is dragged behind a locked gate, her mother presses her body against the gate and cries out, filling the barn with a sound reminiscent of a tornado siren. But the gate doesn't budge. This is the last time she will ever see her calf, and I feel like she realizes it.

Number 70426 continues to call for her baby throughout the afternoon. When she notices me watching, she begins alternating her attention between the gate and me, bellowing with increased urgency. I have to wonder if she is just afraid, or if she is actually pleading for my help.

70426's calf, issued the number 21562, is about to begin a life of intensive milk production. When she is only weeks old, 21562's horns and tail are amputated. No anesthesia is used. I watch as she is muzzled and tied to a post with the same halter rope used on her mother a month earlier. Using a hot iron scoop, a barn worker begins a process called 'disbudding,' literally digging the formative horn buds out of her skull. I'll never forget the sight of the smoke billowing from the calf's head as the hot iron met her skin, coupled with the sizzling sound and smell of seared tissue.

'It's incredibly f***ing painful,' is how my supervisor explains the process to me. As the worker burns into her skull with the device, 21562 attempts to buck, cries out and tries to escape, but in her ad hoc restraints, she can only produce a muffled moan, before she begins to shake, and finally, collapses.

Unfazed, the worker grabs her tail, yanks her back up, and callously digs his thumb and forefinger into her eye sockets, painfully restricting her motion even further, as he resumes his work.

When the horns are fully burned away, she is then 'tail docked.' The worker uses a steel clamp to remove a portion of 21562's tail, slicing through her skin, bone, and nerve endings as she kicks and continues to bellow in distress. When she is finally released from the muzzle, saliva pours from her mouth.

Disbudding is an almost universal mutilation carried out on calves raised in intensive confinement on dairy factory farms. When she matures, 21562 will spend every day in a crowded indoor pen, backed up against hundreds of other cows, each vying for space in this narrow, concrete enclosure. The pens are never properly cleaned, forcing her to live in her own bacteria-laden manure. She will only leave this space when she is herded to the milking parlor, milked for five minutes by an automated machine, and returned to her pen. Unlike the pastoral images stamped on the products in which her milk will be sold, 21562 will never graze outside, and will be deprived of access to sunshine, open space, fresh air, and a normal diet.

Cows at this facility are expected to produce upwards of 80 pounds of milk each day— more than five times what they produce naturally. Milk production is bolstered by a foreign diet of grain, longer hours of artificial light, and the routine use of antibiotics, steroids, and the controversial growth hormone rBST. Above all, her milk production is manipulated through repeated impregnation.(39)

When a cow begins to produce less that 65 pounds of milk a day, she is 'freshened,' meaning artificially inseminated to restimulate lactation, typically as soon as two months after her most recent calving.

Such an intensive breeding regimen coupled with overmilking is known to cause malnutrition, mastitis (a painful udder inflammation that increases pus levels in milk), abomasal displacement (stomach distention), leg spraddling (crippling), and uterine prolapses (inversion of the uterus which reduces blood flow and causes decay).

Number 46570 endured a lifetime under these conditions before succumbing to a crippling joint infection. She developed a bad sore where her back leg repeatedly chafed on her concrete 'bed.' The open wound became impacted with manure until it swelled to the size of a softball, visibly dripping pus from a deep abscess in the center....I checked on 46570 a week later and was dismayed, if not surprised, to learn that she still hadn't received any meaningful veterinary care. Her cloudy eyes were flared open with an intense look I had seen many times before—an expression of unimaginable suffering.

Another week went by and she still lay in the same place. By now, she had become extremely thin, far too weak to even lift her head to drink. I sought out the facility's only veterinarian, who insisted that she might still get up if given time.

[T]here might have been another reason for prolonging her suffering. Recent legislation banned the sale of downers for human consumption, but not for use in animal by-products....[T]his loophole means there's a financial incentive for dairy facilities to withhold humane euthanasia until a downer can be sold to a rendering facility, which will process her into the raw ingredients of products like soap and dog food.

Respite finally came during the third week...in the form of a rendering truck. She lay motionless as a chain was strapped around her leg and she was dragged into the cargo hold.

My eyes followed her until they settled on the nursery pen where I saw 70426's emotional separation from her last calf, 21562.

[T]his cycle of life, death, pain, and profit would continue, not just on this factory farm, but on thousands across the nation.(40)

These are not isolated incidents. I know you want to believe that they are, but they aren't. Every time an investigator goes undercover, these sorts of routine horrors and abuses come to light. Every time.(41)

One of the most well known cases of nonhuman abuse for the purpose of food is the method by which veal calves are "raised" in small, wooden crates which prevent them from even turning around. The babies are deprived of light and iron during their entire short lives in order to produce tender meat. "So intense was their craving for iron that they drank their urine."(42)

> In some West and South African countries, chimpanzees have been hunted for food. The hunting developed into a commercial business—the bush meat trade. Unfortunately, since chimpanzees carry a variant of the human HIV virus, it cannot be ruled out that the virus crossed over to humans due to the butchering of chimpanzees for meat.(43)

> In addition, a live animal trade occurred in West and South Africa. Females were killed and their infants were captured and sold as pets or to the entertainment or medical research industries.(44)

Furthermore, for those who believe "free range" meat is "humane," please watch a video made by University of Texas film student, Neel Parekh, called *Free Range?* at http://vimeo.com/19118301.(45)

"I, for my part, wonder of what sort of feeling,
mind or reason that man was possessed who was first
to pollute his mouth with gore, and to allow his lips to
touch the flesh of a murdered being: who spread his table
with the mangled forms of dead bodies, and claimed as
daily food and dainty dishes what but now were beings
endowed with movement, perception and with voice.
...but for the sake of some little mouthful of flesh,
we deprive a soul of the sun and light,
and of that portion of life and time
it had been born into the world to enjoy."
Plutarch, circa 46-120

"Animals are my friends–and I don't eat my friends."
George Bernard Shaw, 1856-1950

"As Americans get more and more obese, tens of millions
of human beings in the world (including 15 million
children) die from malnutrition, infection and diarrhea."
Kathy Freston, Author

31

Approximately [one] billion people—1/6 of the population—on this planet don't have enough to eat.(46)

[Forty] percent of the world's grain goes to feeding livestock.(47)

In the year 2007 alone, approximately 100 million metric tons of grain and corn was turned into biofuels, which in turn drove up food prices for the global poor by 75 percent, according to a World Bank report; in that same period, 756 million metric tons was fed to chickens, pigs, and other farmed animals.(48)

If [one] in [ten] people around the globe stopped eating animals, it would free up enough food to feed the [one] billion hungry.(49)

One out of every six of our fellow humans has to scrounge for food and feel the ache of an empty stomach every day. And each and every year, tens of millions (15 million of them children) die from starvation-related problems like infections and diarrhea—all this even as Americans get more and more obese.(50)

[I]n a report by Worldwatch Institute called *Underfed and Overfed* their scientists note that 1.2 billion people in the world are underfed and malnourished, while approximately the same number, a different group of 1.2 billion people, are *overfed* and malnourished. And both the hungry and the overweight have high levels of sickness, shortened life expectancies, and lower levels of productivity, albeit for entirely opposite reasons—the overfed tend to die of cancer, heart disease, and diabetes while the underfed tend to die of infectious diseases and waterborne illnesses.(51)

In the United States, more than 95 percent of pigs, chickens, and turkeys never spend any time in pasture, even though these animals were built for greens. The only animals who spend any significant amount of time grazing are cattle (about six months), and even they are crammed together in feedlots for more than half their lives, where they are fed vast quantities of animal feed. It is the business of these factory farms to get the animals as fat as possible as quickly as possible, and this is accomplished by keeping them indoors gorging on animal feed.(52)

There is a direct and measurable relationship between human starvation and the grain being grown for industry. A few years ago, the [United Nation's] special envoy on food, Jean Ziegler, decried the growing production of biofuels: While human beings are starving, he argued, it is a crime against humanity that grains and corns be converted into fuel. He has a point: According to the UN, in 2007 approximately 100 million metric tons of grain and corn was turned into biofuels...which have driven up food prices for the global poor by 75 percent, according to a World Bank report. The *Guardian's* coverage of the report notes that '[r]ising food prices have pushed 100 [million] people worldwide below the poverty line...and have sparked riots from Bangladesh to Egypt."(53)

Despite earnest attempts to give animals a decent, "humane living" by farmers who own family operations, intensive factory farming has taken over the industry. Conscious, sentient nonhuman beings suffer unconscionably due to unnatural rapid growth as a result of steroids and other drugs conducive to skeletal and muscular problems; filthy, inhumane conditions in which they exist; brutal mistreatment by workers; cruel methods of transportation from factory farms to slaughterhouses whereby they are packed on top of each other and crushed; torturous ways by which they are mutilated; and abject disregard for their intrinsic value as sentient living beings.

EarthSave International provided the following recent findings:

1.   The United Nations reports that because of over-fishing, all 17 of the world's major fishing areas have reached or exceeded their natural limits.

2.   Livestock grazing harms roughly 20 percent of all threatened and endangered species in the United States.

3.   On October 12, 1995, the *New York Times* reported, "Burning in the Amazon appears to be approaching the worst levels ever." Clearing forests to create cattle pasture is a principal cause of fires.

4.   Thirty-eight percent of world grain production, 70 percent of United States grain, and one-third of the world's fish catch are fed directly to livestock. In Mexico, where 22 percent of citizens suffer from malnutrition, 30 percent of all grain is fed to livestock.

5.   Producing one pound of feedlot beef takes up to 2,500 gallons of water and about 12 pounds of grain. It takes six pounds of grain and up to 660 gallons of water to produce one pound of chicken. To produce one egg requires three gallons of water.(54)

Clothing and other Consumer Products

*"All tyranny needs to gain a foothold is for people of good
conscience to remain silent."*
Thomas Jefferson, 1743-1826

Capturing and tormenting sentient nonhuman beings
for their fur, wool, leather, feathers, et al. (human tyranny
over nonhumans) remains unnecessary because synthetic
materials that provide warmth and fashionable styles are
readily available—at much lower prices. Each and every
article of attire or product made from a sentient nonhuman
being is the result of a lifetime of *unnecessary* suffering of
that innocent being. (See live video footage of undercover
investigations at www.peta.org.)

Fur bearing beings die after hours or days spent in
agony with a leg caught in a steel toothed trap. They
> spend their entire lives confined to cramped,
> filthy, wire cages. Fur farmers use the
> cheapest, cruelest methods of killing
> available including suffocation,
> electrocution, gas, and poison. More than
> half the fur in the U.S. comes from China
> where millions of dogs and cats are

bludgeoned, hanged, bled to death, and often skinned alive for their fur.(55)

If [sheep who remain gentle beings] were left alone and not genetically manipulated, [they] would grow just enough wool to protect themselves from temperature extremes. The fleece provides effective insulation against both cold and heat. Shearers are usually paid by volume, not by the hour, which encourages fast work without regard for the welfare of the sheep. Says one eyewitness, '[T]he shearing shed must be one of the worst places in the world for cruelty to animals...I have seen shearers punch sheep with their shears or their fists until the sheep's nose bled. I have seen sheep with half their faces shorn off ...'(56)

Within weeks of birth, lambs' ears are hole-punched, their tails are chopped off, and the males are castrated without anesthetics. Male lambs are castrated when they are between [two] and [eight] weeks old, either by making an incision and cutting their testicles out or with a rubber ring used to cut off blood supply—one of the most painful methods of castration possible. Every year, hundreds of lambs die before the age of [eight] weeks from exposure or starvation, and mature sheep die every year from disease, lack of shelter, and neglect.(57)

Much of the world's wool comes from the merino sheep of Australia

who are specifically bred to have wrinkly skin which creates more wool per each being. This unnatural overload of wool causes many sheep to collapse and even die of heat exhaustion during hot months, and the wrinkles collect urine and moisture which attract flies who lay eggs in the folds of the sheep's skin.(58)

In order to prevent 'flystrike,' ranchers perform a gruesome, barbaric procedure called 'mulesing,' a mutilation process

in which they force live sheep onto their backs, restrain their legs between metal bars, and, often without painkillers, carve huge chunks of skin away from the victims' backsides.(59)

Alternatively,

ranchers attach clamps to the sheep's flesh until the skin dies and sloughs off. Mulesing is a crude attempt to create smoother skin that won't collect moisture, but the exposed, bloody wounds often become infected or flystruck. Many sheep who have undergone mulesing still suffer slow, agonizing deaths from flystrike.(60)

Nonhuman beings

who are trapped in the wild can suffer for days from blood loss, shock, dehydration, frostbite, gangrene, and attacks by predators. They may be caught in steel-jaw traps that slam down on their legs, often cutting to the bone [such as] Conibear traps which crush their necks with 90 pounds of pressure per square inch or water-set traps which leave beavers, muskrats, and other [innocent, sentient beings] struggling for more than nine agonizing minutes before drowning.(61)

Most leather comes from developing countries such as India and China.

In India, a PETA investigation found that workers break cows' tails, and rub chili peppers and tobacco into their eyes in order to force them to get up and walk after they collapse from exhaustion on the way to the slaughterhouse.(62)

Research and Experimentation

"How smart does a chimp have to be
before killing him constitutes murder?"
Carl Sagan, 1934-1996

Sentient beings are tortured in military experimentation. Examples of our tax dollars at work follow. A flight simulator known as Primate Equilibrium Platform (PEP) consists of a platform used to simulate an airplane flight. Starved monkeys are subjected to electric shocks in order to test how radiation and chemical warfare agents including Soman (nerve gas) affect their ability to fly.(63)

The standard training procedure for the PEP is described in a Brooks Air Force Base publication entitled 'Training Procedure for Primate Equilibrium Platform'....Phase II (stick adaptation): The monkeys are restrained in the PEP chair. The chair is tipped forward and the monkeys are given electric shocks. This causes the monkey to 'turn in the chair or bite the platform...This behavior is redirected toward the [experimenter's] gloved hand which is placed directly over the control stick.' Touching the hand results in the shock being stopped, and the monkey (who has not been fed that day) is given a raisin. This happens to each money one hundred times a day for between five and eight days....Phase IV...Shocks are manually given at approximately every three or four seconds for a 0.5 second duration....After this period, training continues for another twenty days....All this training, involving thousands of electric shocks, is only preliminary to the real experiment.(64)

Dr. Donald Barnes, principal investigator of the United States Air Force School of Aerospace Medicine in charge of the experiments with PEP at Brooks Air Force Base, resigned and became a strong opponent of animal experimentation although PEP experiments continued.(65)

Dr. Barnes wrote,

I...now acknowledge my eagerness to accept assurances from those in command that we were, in fact, providing a real service to the U.S. Air Force, and, hence, to the defense of the free world. I used those assurances as blinkers...they did serve to protect me from the insecurities associated with the potential loss of status and income...And then, one day, the blinkers slipped off, and I found myself in a very serious confrontation with Dr. Roy DeHart, Commander, U.S. Air Force School of Aerospace Medicine. I tried to point out that, given a nuclear confrontation, it is highly unlikely that operational commanders will go to charts and figures based upon data from the rhesus monkey to gain estimates of probable force strength or second strike capability. Dr. DeHart insisted that the data will be invaluable, asserting, 'They don't know the data are based on animals studies.'(66)

At the Armed Forces Radiobiology Research Institute in Bethesda, Maryland, rhesus monkeys are "trained" to run on treadmills until death to conduct military research on lethal doses of gamma-neutron radiation.(67)

Under the direction of the United States Amy Medical Bioengineering Research and Development Laboratory at Fort Detrick, in Frederick, Maryland, researchers fed 60 beagle dogs varied doses of the explosive TNT. The dogs were given the TNT capsules every day for six months. Symptoms observed included dehydration, emaciation, anemia, jaundice, low body temperature, discolored urine and feces, diarrhea, loss of appetite and weight loss,

43

enlarged livers, kidneys and spleen, and the beagles became uncoordinated. One female was 'found to be moribund (dying)' during week 14 and was killed; another was found dead during week 16.(68)

"One day the world will look upon research on animals as it now looks upon research on human beings."

Leonardo Da Vinci

Additionally, consumer products such as cosmetics and pharmaceuticals fare no better for the innocent, sentient nonhuman victims.

Cosmetic and other substances are tested in animals' eyes. The Draize eye irritancy tests were first used in the 1940s, when J. H. Draize, working for the Food and Drug Administration, developed a scale for assessing how irritating a substance is when placed in rabbits' eyes. The animals are usually placed in holding devices from which only their heads protrude. This prevents them from scratching or rubbing their eyes. A test substance (such as bleach, shampoo, or ink) is then placed in one eye of each rabbit. The method used is to pull out the lower eyelid and place the substance into the small 'cup' thus formed. The eye is then held closed. Sometimes the application is repeated. The rabbits are observed for eye swelling, ulceration, infection, and bleeding. The studies can last up to three weeks. One researcher employed by a large chemical company has described the highest level of reaction as follows:

Total loss of vision due to serious internal injury to cornea of internal structure. Animal holds eye shut urgently. May squeal, claw at eye, jump and try to escape.(69)

In March 1987, Jane Goodall visited SEMA, Inc. in Rockville, Maryland, a federally funded research laboratory.

[Chimpanzees existed in] tiny cages, far gone in depression and despair.

[I]nfant chimpanzees, one or two years old, were crammed, two together, into tiny cages that measured (as I later learned) some twenty-two inches by twenty inches square, and twenty-four inches high. Each cage was inside an 'isolette,' which looked a bit like a micowave oven...

A juvenile female rocked from side to side, sealed off from the outside world. We needed a flashlight to see her properly. A technician was told to open her cage, lift her out. She sat in his arms like a rag doll,

45

listless, apathetic. He did not speak to her. She did not look at him or try to interact with him in any way. She was either drugged, or far gone in despair. Her name, they said, was Barbie.(70)

I am still haunted by the memory of Barbie's eyes, and the eyes of the other chimps I saw that day. They were dull and blank, like the eyes of people who have lost all hope...Chimpanzee children are so like human children, in so many ways. And their emotional needs are the same—both need friendly contact and reassurance and fun and the opportunity to engage in wild bouts of play. And they need love.(71)

I talked about the lives of chimpanzees in the wild, their close family ties, their long and carefree childhood. I described their use of tools, their love of comfort, the rich variety of their diet, and some of our recent insights into the workings of the chimpanzee mind. Then I broached the idea of a workshop, a meeting at which biomedical scientists and veterinarians and technicians from labs could discuss, with field scientists and ethologists and animal welfare advocates, what could be done to improve conditions for the lab chimpanzees.
The workshop took place, but the NIH dropped out and the document outlined what we considered the absolute minimum

requirements for lab chimps as regards cage size, social life, and mental stimulation was largely disregarded by the regulatory body, the U.S. Department of Agriculture." Nevertheless, the document proved useful over the years because it included views of scientists and lab personnel, not only animal rights advocates.(72)

As of 1999, the SEMA lab changed its name, removed the isolettes, gave the chimpanzees large cages and paired them for all experiments.(73)

Jane Goodall first met JoJo in 1988 in a facility owned by New York University's Laboratory for Experimental Medicine and Surgery in Primates— LEMSIP.

It was the first time I had visited *adult* chimpanzees in a lab. The veterinarian, Dr. Jim Mahoney, introduced me. 'JoJo's very gentle,' he said, as he walked away between the rows of cages, five on each side of the bleak, harshly lit underground room. I knelt down in front of JoJo, and he reached as much of his hand as he could between the thick bars that formed a barrier between us. The bars were all around him, on every side, above and below. He had already been in this tiny prison for at least ten years; ten years of utter boredom interspersed with periods of fear and pain. There was nothing in his cage save an old motor tire for him to sit on. And he had no opportunity to contact others of his kind. I looked into his eyes. There was no hatred there, only a sort of gratitude because I stopped to talk to him, helped to break the terrible grinding monotony of the day. Gently, he groomed the ridges where my nails pressed against the thin rubber of the gloves I had been given, along with mask and paper cap. I pushed my hand in between the bars and, lip smacking, he groomed the hairs on the back of my wrist, peeling the glove down.(74)

JoJo's mother had been shot in Africa. Could he remember that life? I wondered. Did he sometimes dream of the great trees with the breeze rustling through the canopy, the birds singing, the comfort of his mother's arms? I thought of David Greybeard and the other chimpanzees of Gombe. I looked again at JoJo as he groomed me, and my vision blurred. Not for him the freedom to choose each day how he would spend his time and where and with whom. There was no comfort for him of soft forest floor or leafy nest, high in the treetops. And the sounds of nature were gone too, the tumbling of the streams, the roar of the waterfall through the dim greens and browns of the forest world, the wind rustling and sighing in the branches, the scuttlings of little creatures moving through the leaves, the chimpanzee calls rising, so clear, from the distant hills.(75)

JoJo has lost his world long, long ago. Now he was in a world of our choosing, a world that was hard and cold and bleak, concrete and steel, clanging doors, and the deafening volume of chimpanzee calls confined in underground rooms. Horrible sounds. A world where there were no windows, nothing to look at, nothing to play with. There was no comfort of gently grooming fingers, no friend to embrace and kiss in joyous morning greeting, no chance to impress with a magnificent display of malehood. JoJo had committed no crime, yet he was imprisoned, for life. The shame I felt was because I was human. Very gently JoJo reached out through the bars and touched my cheek where the tears ran down into my mask. He sniffed his finger, looked briefly into my eyes, went on grooming my wrist. I think Saint Francis stood beside us, and he too was weeping.(76)

As of 1999, JoJo retired to a sanctuary in California when LEMSIP closed and many other chimps were placed in sanctuaries throughout North America.(77)

49

"Atrocities are no less atrocities when they occur in laboratories and are called research."

George Bernard Shaw

Entertainment

"If [man] is not to stifle his human feelings,
he must practice kindness towards animals,
for he who is cruel to animals
becomes hard also in his dealings with men.
We can judge the heart of a man
by his treatment of animals."
Immanuel Kant, 1724-1804

The entertainment industry including fighting events, circuses and zoos has attempted to defend repugnant use of sentient nonhuman beings. Trainers beat, hit, poke, prod, and jab their vulnerable, fearful victims with whips, tight collars, muzzles, electric prods, bull hooks, and other painful methods of punishment and deprivation in order to break their spirit. It remains *unnecessary* to imprison sentient nonhuman beings in small cages for human beings to stare at, to train them to fight or to torment and to abuse them to force them to learn unnatural tricks.

One of the worst records of inhumanity exists in the history of the Ringling Brothers and Barnum & Bailey Circus owned by Feld Entertainment.

> Tom Rider, a former Ringling Bros. Worker, has sharply criticized practices of training. He claims that the lions and tigers are only docile because 'the cats are beat into submission as babies.'(78)

> PETA reported that a whistleblower told them that Clyde [a charismatic two year old lion who represented one of the youngest performers of the circus] died in a poorly ventilated boxcar while traveling in high heat through the Mojave Desert.(79)

> An examination of records from 1990 to 2002 shows that Ringling was cited every year during this period by the USDA's Animal Care division. Despite these citations, the Feld Entertainment website continued to advertise that 'in all aspects of animal care and safety, Ringling Bros. Meets or exceeds all federal animal welfare standards set by the United States Department of Agriculture (USDA) under the Animal Welfare Act. (This statement was later revised to say, 'In all aspects of animal care and safety, Ringling Bros.

Meets all federal animal welfare standards.')(80)

♥ Self Awareness and Equal Consideration

A sentient being *is* a being with an interest in continuing to live, who desires, prefers, or wants to continue to live....A sentient being is self-aware in that she knows that it is she, and not another, who is feeling pain and suffering.(81)

Sentience is necessary to have interests at all....But if a being is sentient, this is sufficient to be self-aware and to have an interest in continued existence.(82)

Cognitive characteristics beyond sentience cannot represent additional necessary and sufficient conditions for personhood. Things do not possess sentience. No matter how much you torture things, objects cannot feel pain. No matter how much you love things, objects cannot return the emotion of love. Things do not smile or cry. If characteristics such as the abilities to reason and to talk were necessary for personhood, then human infants and many mentally challenged individuals (who cannot reason or talk in a humanlike way) must be regarded as property—

which is ridiculous at best. Accordingly, sentience represents the exclusive, necessary and sufficient requirement for personhood.

> The position that cognitive characteristics beyond sentience or humanlike versions of these characteristics are morally more important than other characteristics begs the question from the outset. Why is the ability to do calculus morally better than the ability to fly with your wings? Why is the ability to recognize yourself in a mirror morally better than your ability to recognize yourself in a scent that you left on a bush? Moreover, there is no logical relationship between differences in cognitive characteristics and the issue of animal use, although these differences may be relevant for some purposes.(83)

> Moreover, the proposition that humans have mental characteristics wholly absent in animals in inconsistent with the theory of evolution. Darwin maintained that there are no uniquely human characteristics: '[T]he difference in mind between man and the higher animals, great as it is, is certainly one of degree and not of kind.' Animals are able to think, and possess many of the same emotional responses as do humans: '[T]he senses and intuitions, the various emotions

and faculties, such as love, memory, attention, curiosity, imitation, reason, &c., of which man boasts, may be found in an incipient, or even sometimes in a well-developed condition, in the lower animals.' Darwin noted that 'associated animals have a feeling of love for each other' and that animals 'certainly sympathize with each other's distress or danger.'(84)

Professor Singer popularized the term "speciesism(85)" that supports the concept of equal consideration. As Professor Singer explains in several editions of *Animal Liberation*, "speciesism," discrimination based on species, is identical to discrimination based on race, color, national origin, religion, gender, age, disability, etcetera.

Professor Francione explains,

The application of the principle of equal consideration similarly failed in the context of North American slavery, which allowed some humans to treat others as property. The institution of human slavery was structurally identical to the institution of animal ownership. Because a human slave was regarded as property, the slave owner was able to disregard all of the slave's interests if it was economically beneficial to do so, and the law generally deferred to the slave owner's judgment as to the value of the slave. As chattel property, slaves could be sold, willed, insured, mortgaged, and seized in payment of the owner's debts. Slave owners could inflict severe punishments on slaves for virtually any reason. Those who intentionally or negligently injured another's slave were liable to the owner in an action for damage to property. Slaves could not enter into contracts, own property, sue or be sued, or live as free persons with basic rights and duties.(86)

Accordingly, all sentient beings, regardless of race, color, national origin, religion, gender, age, disability, sexual orientation, or species, deserve the rights to life, liberty and freedom not to be used as commodities or resources of other sentient beings.

"The love for all living creatures is the most noble
attribute of man."
Charles Darwin, 1809–1882

"It's a matter of taking the side
of the weak against the strong,
something the best of people have always done."
Harriet Beecher Stowe, 1811-1896

"If you talk to the animals, they will talk with you;
and you will know each other.
If you do not talk to them, you will not know them;
and what you do not know, you will fear.
What one fears, one destroys."
Chief Dan George, 1899-1981

"Compassion is a muscle that gets stronger with use,
and the regular exercise of choosing
kindness over cruelty...change[s] us."
Jonathan Safran Foer, Author

3 / The Special Case of Military War Dogs and Law Enforcement Service Dogs

Since World War I, Military War dogs have been fighting for United States Constitutional Rights although they *do not possess any Rights themselves.* Additionally, law enforcement service dogs perform a vital role, as police assistants, in maintaining law and order, and, as employees of the United States Department of Homeland Security, in providing for our nation's security as well as the safety of citizens.

In the interest of Justice, Law, Equity and Fairness, we must *either* prohibit the use of sentient nonhuman beings in military and law enforcement services *or* bestow the status of personhood on them.

4 / Spirituality, Religion and Philosophy

♥ Spiritual Words of Wisdom throughout Time

*"Whenever we cause suffering or death to any other being,
we cause suffering in the Great Life Force."*
Shik Po Chih

*"One is dearest to God who has no enemies
among the living beings,
who is nonviolent to all creatures."*
Bhagavad Gita, Krishna

*"All beings tremble before violence.
All fear death.
All love life."*
Siddhartha Gautama Buddha, circa 563-483 BC

"May all that have life be delivered from suffering."
Siddhartha Gautama Buddha

Beloved, let us love one another, for love is from God,
and whoever loves has been born of God and knows God.
(or words to this effect)
English language of Biblical scripture 1 John 4:7

No one has ever seen God; if we love one another,
God abides in us and his love is perfected in us.
(or words to this effect)
English language of Biblical scripture 1 John 4:12

"If you have men who will exclude any of God's creatures
from the shelter of compassion and pity,
you will have men who will deal likewise
with their fellow men."
Saint Francis of Assisi, 1191-1226

"In my mind, the life of a lamb is no less precious
than that of a human being.
The more helpless the creature,
the more it is entitled to protection by man
from the cruelty of man."
Mahatma Gandhi, 1869-1948

"The greatness of a nation and its moral progress
can be judged by the way its animals are treated."
Mahatma Gandhi

"We are all God's creatures—
that we pray to God for mercy and justice,
while we continue to eat the flesh of animals
that are slaughtered on our account,
is not consistent."
Isaac Bashevis Singer, Nobel Peace Prize laureate,
1902-1991

"Animals, too, are God's creatures...
Certainly, a sort of industrial use of creatures,
so that geese are fed in such a way as to produce as large
a liver as possible, or hens live so packed together
that they become just caricatures of birds,
this degrading of living creatures to a commodity
seems to me in fact to contradict the relationship of
mutuality that comes across in the Bible."
Pope Benedict XVI

♥ Christianity

In Genesis 1:26, the Bible states that God gave humans "dominion over creatures." First, no one really knows the *exact meaning* of the *original intent* of Biblical language. Much of the Bible was written many decades after the events occurred. If we study Aramaic, Hebrew, Greek and Latin, we may translate it, but languages never translate perfectly with respect to *meaning and intention.* For example, "[M]any Hebrew scholars believe the word 'dominion' is a very poor translation of the original Hebrew word *v'yirdu* which actually meant to *rule over;* as a wise king rules over his subjects, *with care and respect.* It implied a sense of responsibility and enlightened stewardship."(87) Likewise, the use of the English word "fear" when translated *as accurately as possible* through the languages is "awe." Fear may include dread and worry, but not reverence, wonder and admiration. Nevertheless, many English translations of countless versions of the Bible contain the phraseology, "fear God."

The Lord has dominion over us all. Seemingly, all animals remain equal in the eyes of the Lord. For example, with respect to the Tenth Plague, Biblical scripture Exodus 12:29 contains English words to the effect: the Lord struck down *all the firstborn males* in the land of Egypt, from the first born of Pharaoh who sat on his throne to the firstborn of the captive who was in the dungeon, and all the firstborn of the livestock; and Exodus 13:15 contains English words to the effect: the Lord killed all the firstborn males in the land of Egypt, both the firstborn of humans and the firstborn of nonhumans.

More importantly, if it were true that God gave human beings "dominion over creatures," then creatures must require *more protection*, not less.

Most significantly, it remains irrelevant if/that human beings used and consumed nonhuman beings (and owned slaves, and disregarded rights of women) during Biblical times because twenty-first century American civilization certainly has the intellectual ability as a modern society to continue to advance morally with regard to animal rights (or any other issue) just as nineteenth century Americans abolished slavery and twentieth century Americans achieved women's suffrage.

5 / The Solution

As Professor Francione advises, veganism is the moral baseline of animal rights. Nonhuman beings should not be used by human beings for food, clothing and other consumer products, research subjects or entertainment. Furthermore, nonhuman beings should not be abused in any way. Sufficient resources exist in the world to utilize suitable substitutes and moral alternatives to animal flesh, dairy, eggs, fur, wool, leather, feathers, testing of drugs and other products as well as entertainment. Veganism is conducive to eliminating unnecessary pain, distress, suffering and disease of nonhuman beings. Since veganism serves as a nutritious, healthful method of eating, incidents of human diseases would decrease.

With respect to food, because it is more efficient to eat grain rather than to feed grain to nonhuman beings and eat nonhuman beings, everyone in the world would have enough to eat if veganism were faithfully practiced.

Veganism represents a rejection of the commodity status of nonhumans and a recognition of their inherent value.(88)

Veganism, which results in a decreased demand for animal products, is much more than a matter of diet, lifestyle, or consumer choice; it is a personal commitment to nonviolence and the abolition of exploitation. A person who agrees that animal use is not morally justified but who continues to consume animal products is similar to those in 1830 who opposed slavery but who continued to own slaves. In a society underpinned by animal exploitation, it is extremely difficult—perhaps impossible—not to be at least indirectly complicit in animal exploitation as consumers, but we can nevertheless be clear that if we are not vegans, we certainly *are* animal exploiters.(89)

"The doctor of the future will give no medicine, but will interest his patients in the care of the human body, in diet, and in the cause and prevention of disease."
Thomas Edison, 1847-1965

66

*"Nothing will benefit human health
and increase chances for survival of life on Earth
as much as the evolution to a vegetarian diet."*
Albert Einstein, 1879–1955

*"Your choice of diet can influence
your long term health prospects
more than any other action you might take."*
Former Surgeon General C. Everett Koop

The following book addresses the most serious problems of our nation and of the world, ie, cancer, heart disease, diabetes, obesity, high cost of health insurance, starvation and malnutrition related diseases of the global poor, animal suffering, global warming, slashing and burning of forests, pollution, depletion of fossil fuels and lack of compassion.

In *Veganist, Lose Weight, Get Healthy, Change the World*, Kathy Freston, Wellness Expert and New York Times bestselling author of *Quantum Wellness*, makes the following ten promises and supports each one with medical and scientific authority, Government statistics and real life testimonies.

1.   Your Body Will Find and Maintain Its Ideal Weight—Effortlessly

2.   You Will Lower Your Risks for Cancer, Heart Disease and Diabetes—and Even Reverse Diseases Already Diagnosed

3.   You Will Live Longer—and Better

4.   You Will Take Yourself Out of Harm's Way

5.   You Will Save Money

6.   You Will Radically Reduce Your Carbon Footprint and Do the Single Best Thing You Can for the Environment

7.   You Will Be Helping Provide Food to the Global Poor

8.   You Will Reduce Animal Suffering

9.   You Will Be Following the Wisdom of the Great Spiritual Traditions

10.   You Will Evolve—and Take the World with You.

"[T]he vast majority—more than 95 percent—of animals people eat are raised in factory farms and not on the old-fashioned family farms of memory. When you eat a plant-based diet,"(90) you make the aforementioned powerful promises to yourself.

6 / Ramifications

♥ Effects of Veganism on Capitalism

How would factory farmers produce profits? They would produce soy, grain and plant products. How would pharmaceutical companies stay in business? They would work with the National Institute of Health (NIH), scientists, medical professionals and relevant organizations to discover, invent and implement alternatives to nonhuman animal testing *which would create or at the very least save jobs.* Regarding research and experimentation, sentient nonhuman beings do not have the same reactions to drugs as human beings; it has been *proven* and remains common knowledge today that nonhuman beings serve as poor research models for human illnesses. "If we want data that will be useful in finding cures for human diseases, we would be better advised to use humans."(91)

With regard to clothing and other consumer products, manufacturers would create synthetic materials such as faux fur, wool, leather, feathers, et al. Circuses, zoos and fighting events would make entertainment changes for the betterment of the entire moral community.

Jane Goodall comments on the social and political implications of change:

> [W]e cannot condone forever the pursuit of unethical, cruel, and destructive behaviors simply because to end them will create problems: would anyone advocate the continuation of concentration camps in order to ensure jobs of those in charge?(92)

Since the origin of this country, the United States government has subsidized farmers. Accordingly, the Abolitionist Theory of Animal Rights should not increase farm subsidies that have existed for over 200 years, but rather would require government reorganization; not additional funding.

♥ Justice, Freedom of Choice and Legislation of Morality

"Our lives begin to end the day we become silent about things that matter."

Dr. Martin Luther King Jr., 1929-1968

Professor Francione advises that veganism, the *abolition of the use of all products derived from sentient nonhuman beings,* can be accomplished through advocacy and education as an incremental change. I agree that advocacy and education remain imperative; however, I believe sentient nonhuman beings have endured far too many decades of abuse, neglect and torture. Like, the abolition of slavery, abolition of animal use must originate in legislation.

But, what about freedom? What about the human beings who enjoy eating flesh? What about the human beings who enjoy wearing fur? What about prostitution, hate speech, drug use, rape, incest, pedophilia, slavery and murder? The answer is simple...Legislation. *Morality has always been legislated.*

"If we do not do something to help these creatures,
we make a mockery of the whole concept of justice."
Jane Goodall

♥ The Role of Humanity

What is the role of humans, the supposedly most intellectually sophisticated, kind, tender, merciful, civilized and refined group of animals? Is it not to protect and to care for the lower animals with respect and kindness with a "sense of responsibility and enlightened stewardship?"

Jane Goodall opines,

> To me, cruelty is the worst of human sins. Once we accept that a living creature has feelings and suffers pain, then if we knowingly and deliberately inflict suffering on that creature we are equally guilty. Whether it be human or animal we brutalize *ourselves*. It is not always an easy message to get across.(93)

> We still have a long way to go. But we are moving in the right direction. If only we can overcome cruelty, to human and animal, with love and compassion we shall stand on the threshold of a new era in human moral and spiritual evolution—and realize, at last, our most unique quality; humanity.(94)

Conclusion

"Only if we understand can we care.
Only if we care will we help.
Only if we help shall they be saved."
Jane Goodall

The only *effective* way to protect the interests of sentient nonhuman beings is to abolish the use of all animal products.

Each and every human act of compassion makes a difference to one nonhuman life.

‡ Avoid skin, flesh, milk and eggs derived from sentient nonhuman beings.

‡ Purchase faux fur, wool, leather, feathers, and other synthetic materials.

‡ Boycott *anything and everything* that is tested on sentient nonhuman beings.

‡ Boycott events in which sentient nonhuman beings serve as subjects of entertainment.

If we're not part of the solution, we're part of the problem.

After Word

Since the Abolitionist Theory of Animal Rights is based on pure logic, it is not arguable.

All living beings possess sentience (the capability of feeling; consciousness).
Sentience is the exclusive, necessary and sufficient condition for the possession of rights to life, liberty and freedom not to be used as commodities or resources of other living beings.
Nonhuman beings are living beings.
Therefore, nonhuman living beings possess the rights to life, liberty and freedom not to be used as commodities or resources of other living beings.

We know the second premise is true because in order to possess the capability of feeling or consciousness, beings must have nervous systems. Evidence that animals have nervous systems exists; however, plants, vehicles, furniture, clothing, carpet, consumer products, et al. do not have nervous systems.

76

In addition, we know we cannot include the ability to reason as a premise because it would be absurd to classify mentally challenged individuals and infants as property.

The Truth:

Animals are regarded as property due to discrimination based on species just as blacks were once regarded as property due to racial discrimination. It's only a matter of time before animals possess the status of personhood as members of the moral community like blacks, and species discrimination will be against federal law. The question is not "if," but "when." The basis is economic, and the previous and current federal executive administrations under President Obama are moving away from capitalism (an ideological stage in political socio-economic evolution).

As I discussed in the Forward, the application of Civil Rights and Liberties to Animal Law has already made its debut in federal court. On February 8, 2012, the United States District Court, Southern District of California, decided *TILIKUM, Katina, Corky, Kasatka, and Ulises, five orcas, by their Next Friends, PEOPLE FOR THE ETHICAL TREATMENT OF ANIMALS, INC., Richard "Ric" O'Barry, Ingrid N. Visser, Ph.D., Howard Garrrett, Samantha Berg, and Carol Ray v. SEA WORLD PARKS & ENTERTAINMENT, INC. and Sea World, LLC*, Case No. 3:11-CV-02476-JM-WMC, an action based on the Thirteenth Amendment of the Constitution which prohibits slavery and involuntary servitude. Although the Court dismissed the case for lack of subject matter jurisdiction, the action remains an impermeable representation of inevitable change in societal opinion and federal law.

In the aforementioned case, The Honorable Jeffrey T. Miller of the United States District Court, Southern District of California, erred by overlooking statutory, historical and logical facts.

1. That African American individuals were regarded as property until the Civil Rights Act of 1866 was enacted on April 9, 1866.
2. That the United States Constitutional Amendment XIII was ratified on December 6, 1865.

78

3. That United States Constitutional Amendment XIII applied to property, ie, African American individuals, for several months.

4. That until animals become members of the moral community and the status of personhood is bestowed upon them, they are considered property.

5. That the United States Constitutional Amendment XIII applies to property, ie, sentient nonhuman beings, and specifically *Tilikum, Katina, Corky, Kasatka and Ulises, five orcas,* in 2011, as it applied to blacks in the nineteenth century.

Recently, advocates within the animal liberation movement introduced an innovative concept regarding a "quasi-person/property" classification for nonhuman beings possibly for the reason that nonhuman beings require custodians unless they remain wild. This idea would create a controversy with respect to mentally challenged individuals and infants who would logically represent suitable members of this class.

In sum, there exists only one solution: Personhood in order to afford nonhuman beings basic legal rights.

"Nonhuman animals, like all sentient beings,
are entitled to basic legal rights in our society."
Animal Legal Defense Fund

Notes

1. Thomas F. X. Noble, et al., *Western Civilization, The Continuing Experiment, Volume I: to 1715* (Boston: Houghton Mifflin Company, 1994) 141.

2. Thomas F. X. Noble, et al., *Western Civilization, The Continuing Experiment, Volume II: since 1560* (Boston: Houghton Mifflin Company, 1994) 708, 710.

3. Noble Volume I 141.

4. Noble Volume I 218.

5. Noble Volume I 444.

6. Noble Volume II 941, 943.

7. Tom L. Beauchamp, et al., *The Human Use of Animals, Case Studies in Ethical Choice* (Oxford: Oxford University Press, 2008) 4.

8. Beauchamp 4.

9. Peter Singer, *Animal Liberation, The Definitive Classic of the Animal Movement* (New York: HarperCollins Publishers, 2009). (latest edition)

10. This book contains voluminous quotations from Professor Francione's writings because paraphrasing or rewriting perfect, expert language would only serve to denigrate significant, logical arguments. (Likewise, it contains comprehensive quotations of personal accounts of

undercover investigators and same of Jane Goodall to preserve original, poignant events.)

11. Beauchamp 13.

12. Beauchamp 13.

13. Jane Goodall, *Through a Window, My Thirty Years with the Chimpanzees of Gombe* (New York: Soko Publications Limited, 1990) xi.

14. Singer 11.

15. Singer 8.

16. Singer 11.

17. Singer 14.

18. Gary Francione, *Animals as Persons, Essays on the Abolition of Animal Exploitation* (New York: Columbia University Press, 2008) ix.

19. Francione x-xi.

20. Kathy Freston, *Veganist, Lose Weight, Get Healthy, Change the World* (New York: Weinstein Books, 2011).

21. Francione xiii.

22. Francione 9.

23. Francione 16.

24. Francione 39-40.

25. Francione 48.

26. Francione 69.

27. Francione 76.

28. Francione 10.

29. Francione 109.

30. Francione 14-15.

31. Francione 7.

32. Francione 8.

33. Singer 119.

34. Beauchamp 47.

35. Beauchamp 47.

36. Beauchamp 47-48.

37. Freston 176-181.

38. Freston 183-184.

39. Freston 186-189.

40. Freston 189-191.

41. Freston 154.

42. Jane Goodal, *Reason for Hope, A Spiritual Journey* (New York: Soko Publications Limited, 1999) 222.

43. Goodall, *Reason for Hope* 207.

44. Goodall, *Reason for Hope* 207.

45. Freston 192.

46. Freston 158.

47. Freston 158.

48. Freston 158.

49. Freston 158

50. Freston 159.

51. Freston 159.

52. Freston 162.

53. Freston 162.

54. Doreen Virtue, *Eating in the Light* (Carlsbad, California: Hay House, Inc., 2001) 125-127.

55. www.peta.org.

56. www.peta.org.

57. www.peta.org.

58. www.peta.org.

59. www.peta.org.

60. www.peta.org.

61. www.peta.org.

62. www.peta.org.

63. Singer 25.

64. Singer 26-27.

65. Singer 28.

66. Singer 28.

67. Singer 213.

68. Singer 30.

69. Singer 54.

70. Goodall, *Reason for Hope* 211.

71. Goodall, *Reason for Hope* 211-212.

72. Goodall, *Reason for Hope* 213-214.

73. Goodall, *Reason for Hope* 227.

74. Goodall, *Reason for Hope* 215-216.

75. Goodall, *Reason for Hope* 216.

76. Goodall, *Reason for Hope* 216-217.

77. Goodall, *Reason for Hope* 227.

78. Beauchamp 126.

79. Beauchamp 123.

80. Beauchamp 123.

81. Francione 10-11.

82. Francione 11.

83. Francione 11-12.

84. Francione 55.

85. This idea was first advanced by Richard Ryder. Beauchamp 18.

86. Francione 46.

87. Goodall, *Reason for Hope* 272.

88. Francione 109.

89. Francione 16-17.

90. Freston 193.

91. Francione 64.

92. Goodall, *Reason for Hope* 241-242.

93. Goodall, *Reason for Hope* 225.

94. Goodall, *Reason for Hope* 227.

Works Cited

Books

Beauchamp, Tom L., et al., *The Human Use of Animals, Case Studies in Ethical Choice*. Oxford: Oxford University Press, 2008.

Francione, Gary L., *Animals as Persons, Essays on the Abolition of Animal Exploitation*. New York: Columbia University Press, 2008.

Freston, Kathy, *Veganist, Lose Weight, Get Healthy, Change the World*. New York: Weinstein Books, 2011.

Goodall, Jane with Phillip Berman, *Reason for Hope, A Spiritual Journey*. New York: Soko Publications Limited, 1999.

Goodall, Jane, *Through a Window, My Thirty Years with the Chimpanzees of Gombe*. New York: Soko Publications Limited, 1990.

Noble, Thomas F. X., et al., *Western Civilization, The Continuing Experiment, Volume I: to 1715*. Boston: Houghton Mifflin Company, 1994.

Noble, Thomas F. X., et al., *Western Civilization, The Continuing Experiment, Volume II: since 1560*. Boston: Houghton Mifflin Company, 1994.

Singer, Peter, *Animal Liberation, The Definitive Classic of the Animal Movement*. New York: Harper-Collins Publishers, 2009.

Virtue, Doreen, *Eating in the Light*. Carlsbad, California: Hay House, Inc., 2001.

Websites

Francione, Gary L., www.AbolitionistApproach.com.

Mercy for Animals, www.chooseveg.com.

Parekh, Neel, http://vimeo.com/19118301.

People for the Ethical Treatment of Animals, www.peta.org.

About the Author

Carol Elizabeth Mosca graduated from the University of Virginia and has worked in the legal field most of her professional life. For the past several years, she has focused her professional endeavors on animal rights advocacy with emphasis on federal animal rights legislation and social responsibility education within local school districts of the United States. Presently, she prepares to study law, with concentration in Constitutional Law and Animal Rights, in order to continue her work in the Animal Rights legal and legislative arenas to her full potential.

You may contact Carol Elizabeth Mosca directly at justice4sentience@gmail.com or 386-878-1252 *anytime*.

ISBN 978-1-484-15888-3

www.ingramcontent.com/pod-product-compliance
Lightning Source LLC
Chambersburg PA
CBHW051337170526
45166CB00002B/854